PUBLISHED B`
JC Phelps
Edy's Old-Fashioned C
Copyright © 2020 by JC Phelps

NewPub Binding, USA

Edy's Old-Fashioned Cookbook

(Mom's Cookbook)

Foreword
Written by JC Phelps

This cookbook is a labor of love in memory of my mother, Edy. She was the center of my family, so it was a terrible blow to us all when she passed away in 2005. I did everything I could to hang on, and this cookbook is one of the results of that hanging on. Now, it's fifteen years later, and I'm redoing the cookbook once again.

Mom had been working on this cookbook for years. A worn, blue folder held these recipes and other musings of hers. It was that folder she would point me to first whenever I needed a recipe. Eventually, I would find what I was looking for among the small scraps of paper in my mother's handwriting. There was no focused organization to the recipes, so it could take a while to sift through them.

We all have things we want to do in our lives that may never get done, and this cookbook was one of my mothers. She'd told me all I needed to do was to put the recipes into the computer. Shortly after she passed away, I finally decided to get it done. She was never happy in front of the computer and hoped I would take an interest in her cookbook. It took her passing for me to realize how I'd neglected her in some ways.

I remember having trouble picking and choosing the right recipes to include and lamenting that Mom was not around to help me. I know she had many more recipes stored in her head and words of wisdom she wanted to share. As for me, this is me hanging on and sharing my mother with all of you.

To quote my mother's own preface - Thanks, Mom. You taught me everything I know. I love you, Mom.

Preface
Written by Edy Phelps

The recipes you are about to embark upon are some of my favorite recipes. These are the ones I always fall back on. Although I like trying new and different things, these come the easiest to me and seem to all be pleasing to my family and friends. It is always fun to adventure into the unknown, but I find myself more confident with my old stand-bys.

This is my treasured collection of family favorites that I would like to share with everyone. All of these recipes have come from my family and friends through the years of cooking and baking.

I am a simple cooker and baker, yet enjoy the praises from all in my cookery.

This book is dedicated to the memory of my mother.

"Mom, give me the recipe for your cookies."

"Well hon, it's a dash of this and a pinch of that. It's a little of this, but none of that."

Thanks, Mom. You taught me everything I know. I love you, Mom.

Kitchen Chores
by
Edy Phelps

Washing dishes is such a pain,
It's oh so boring and also mundane,
And shortly after you're totally done,
The dirty dishes are back, one by one.

Soon the cupboards are empty,
The sink is full,
The counters are soiled,
And the dishwasher hasn't been touched by
a soul.

So I round them all up and put them away,
And stop to think,
I get to do this every day!

I hate washing dishes!

(She signed it By Mom Only)

I'm thinking this meant that she was the
ONLY one who this poem related to since she
was the only one who washed the dishes.

Beverages

Russian Bear

1/2 oz. Fresh cream

1 oz.　 Creme De Cacoa

2 oz.　 Vodka

Shake well with crushed ice in a shaker.
Pour over ice and serve.

Homemade Wine

2 cans Welchs frozen grape juice

Water

4 cups Sugar

1/4 teaspoon Dry yeast

Add the amount of water suggested on the juice can. Mix all together in a sterilized gallon jar with a narrow enough opening to fit a balloon over. A carboy used for making wine is recommended. Put a large ballon over the opening. Let sit in a cool dark place. The balloon will fill with air as the wine ferments. When the balloon starts to deflate, the wine should be done. This can take several weeks to several months and care should be taken to be sure the balloon does not pop off.

Raisin Wine

2 cans Welches frozen grape juice

3 1/2 cups Sugar

1/4 teaspoon Dry yeast

1 gallon Distilled or boiled water. If using boiled water, cool water to room temperature

1/2 cup Raisins

Mix all together and put into 2 sterilized gallon jars - a carboy used for wine making is recommended. Put a large ballon over the opening. Let sit in a cool dark place. The balloon will fill with air as the wine ferments. When the balloon starts to deflate, the wine should be done. This can take several months and care should be taken to be sure the balloon does not pop off. Strain thoroughly before bottling.

Pina Colada

16 oz. can Coconut Cream

46 oz. Pineapple juice, unsweetened

1 pint Half & Half

1 pint Rum

12 oz. can Frozen lemonade concentrate

Mix well and serve.

Hot Powerful Punch

46 oz. Apple juice

1 1/2 quart Cranapple juice

4 1/2 cups Water

4 Cinnamon sticks

7 Whole cloves

1 pint Brandy (any flavor or brand)

The liquid ingredients, except the brandy, are put in the bottom of a percolator, the spices are put in the basket and allowed to perk like coffee. The flavor will not be ruined by leaving it plugged in. After perking add the 1 pint of brandy.

Irish Cream

Approx. 12.5 oz. Clear liquor such as vodka or white rum. This is approximately half a bottle of a 750 ml bottle.

1 can (14 oz.) Sweetened condensed milk

1 cup Cream or coffee creamer

4 Eggs

2 teaspoons Instant coffee

2 Tablespoons Chocolate syrup

1/2 teaspoon Almond flavoring

Mix together and pour into a bottle. Keep refrigerated. Will last up to two months.

Hot Buttered Rum Mix

1/2 lb. Butter

1/2 lb. Brown sugar

1 teaspoon Cinnamon

1 cup White sugar

1/2 quart Vanilla ice cream

1 teaspoon Nutmeg

Melt butter. Add both sugars and mix well. Add ice cream and spices. Keep frozen.

Chokecherry Wine

1/2 gallon Chokecherries - rinse lightly

1/2 gallon Water

4 cups Sugar

1/4 teaspoon Dry yeast

Mix all together in a sterilized gallon jar with a narrow enough opening to fit a balloon over. A carboy used for making wine is recommended. Put a large ballon over the opening. Let sit in a cool dark place. The balloon will fill with air as the wine ferments. When the balloon starts to deflate, the wine should be done. This can take several weeks to several months and care should be taken to be sure the balloon does not pop off. Strain liquid before bottling.

Old Fashioned Recipes

This recipe book is one thing I have always wanted to do. For the past 20 years I have put it on the back burner and now my recipes are really old-fashioned. Now that my children have grown, I find myself with not any more time, just more patience. I stopped majoring on minors a long time ago.

~Edy Phelps~

Salads

Vegetables

Fruit Salad Dressing

1/2 cup Syrup from canned peaches

1 Tablespoon Sugar

2 Egg yolks, well beaten

1/2 teaspoon Salt

1 1/2 teaspoon Lemon juice

1/8 teaspoon Paprika

Heat peach syrup. In a separate bowl combine egg yolks, salt, sugar and paprika. Add peach syrup slowly, stirring constantly. Cook over hot water (double boiler) until thick and smooth. Remove from heat and slowly add lemon juice, making sure to mix thoroughly. Chill. If desired, other juices may be substituted for peach syrup. Sweeten to taste.

Cheese Peach Salad

1 cup Cottage cheese

1/8 teaspoon Salt

6 halves cooked peaches

Fruit salad dressing above

24 Salted, chopped almonds

Grated rind of 1/2 an orange

Paprika to decorate

Cheese Pear Salad

6 cooked pear halves

1 cup Pear juice

1 cup Cottage cheese

2 Tablespoons Sweet Cream

Salt to taste

Red food coloring for decoration

Combine all ingredients and serve.

Cottage Cheese Dressing

1 small container Creamed cottage cheese

1/4 cup Chopped green pepper

1/4 cup Onion, diced

1/4 cup Tomato, diced

1/4 cup Celery, diced

1/4 cup Mayonnaise

Mix together and serve on a lettuce leaf. Salt to taste.

Salad Dressing

1/2 cup Ketchup

1/2 cup Vegetable oil

1/2 cup Sugar

1/3 cup Vinegar

Dash Worcestershire sauce

Dash Salt

Combine all ingredients into a bottle. Shake well and refrigerate.

French Dressing

2 teaspoons Salt

1/2 teaspoon Pepper

1/4 cup Sugar

1 10 oz. can Tomato soup

1 Tablespoon Dry mustard

1 Tablespoon Paprika

1 1.75 package Pectin

1/2 cup Vinegar

1 1/2 cup Salad oil

1 teaspoon Minced onion

1 clove Garlic

1 Tablespoon Worcestershire sauce

Combine all ingredients into a bottle. Shake well and refrigerate.

Three Bean Salad

1 can Green beans

1 can Yellow beans

1 can Red kidney beans

1 Onion, thinly sliced

1/2 cup Green pepper, diced

3/4 cup Vinegar

1 teaspoon Salt

1 teaspoon Celery salt

1/2 teaspoon Pepper

1/4 cup Salad oil

Cook the beans and cool. Add remaining ingredients and chill over night.

Macaroni Salad

2 cups Cooked macaroni

1 can Tuna

1/2 cup Salad dressing (Miracle Whip)

1 cup Cooked peas

1 Onion, chopped

1/2 cup Grated cheese

1/2 cup Celery, chopped

Mix all together in a bowl. Serve as a side dish with almost any meal.

Pork Dressing

1 16 oz. jar Sauerkraut

1 cup Rice

1 Onion, diced

1/2 cup Celery, diced

1 teaspoon Celery salt

Mix all ingredients into the bottom of a baking dish and cook under a pork roast.

Edy's Barbecue Sauce

1/2 cup Water

1/2 cup Vinegar

6 oz. Tomato paste

3/4 cup Water

1 Tablespoon Maple flavoring

3/4 cup Sugar

1 1/2 teaspoon Onion salt

1 teaspoon Garlic salt

1/4 teaspoon Chili powder

1/8 to 1/4 cup Heinz 57 Sauce

Combine all ingredients into a sauce pan. Bring to a full boil, then reduce to a simmer. Simmer for 5 to 10 minutes before putting on meat.

Salsa
(Canning recipe)

4 cups Tomatoes, peeled, cored, and chopped

2 cups Green peppers, seeded and chopped

1 cup Hot pepper of your choice, diced

3/4 cup Onion, chopped

1 1/2 teaspoon Salt

2 cloves Garlic, finely chopped

1 1/2 cups Apple cider vinegar

Combine all ingredients into a pot. Bring to a boil, lower heat and simmer for 20 minutes. Pour into hot jars and process in a water bath for 30 minutes.

Potato Dumplings

8-10 Potatoes, peeled and boiled

1 teaspoon Baking powder

1/2 teaspoon Salt

Flour

Grind boiled potatoes. Add baking powder, salt and enough flour to make balls. Make into golf ball sized balls and drop into boiling ham juice. Serve with melted butter.

World Famous Duchess Potatoes

(Recipe courtesy of Elk Creek Steakhouse. This recipe is no longer in use at the restaurant as it changed hands and the new owners changed the recipe. It's too bad since this is one of the best ways to eat potatoes.)

Pot Luck Size	Smaller Size
5 lb. Sour cream	2 cups Sour cream
1 gallon Milk	3 1/8 cups Milk
1 teaspoon Tobasco	1-2 dashes Tobasco
1 teaspoon dashes Worcestershire	1-2 dashes Worcestershire
1 Tablespoon White Pepper	1/2 teaspoon White pepper
1 Tablespoon Salt	1/2 teaspoon Salt
3 pounds Bacon	3/4 pound Bacon
2 Onions, diced	1/2 Onion, diced
3 Green peppers, diced	3/4 Green pepper, diced
Instant Potatoes	Instant Potatoes
Butter	Butter
Paprika	Paprika

Cook bacon, pepper, and onion. Mix spices with sour cream. Add milk and cooked bacon mixture. Mix in instant potatoes until desired thickness. Don't make it too thick. It should be fairly thin. Transfer to a baking dish and place a few pats of butter on top, then sprinkle with paprika. Bake in a 400° oven for about 10 minutes. The time will depend on how deep your baking dish is. The finished potatoes should be the consistency of well mashed potatoes.

I'll Starve

My dad was kind of from the old-school. He was born in the 1920's. He wanted us to believe that he didn't know how to open a can of soup. On the weekends he expected three meals a day and during the week, breakfast was on the table every morning, his lunch packed, and supper on the table when he came home from work.

One day, Mom had gone to town. Probably to buy groceries. She left a can of soup, a kettle, and a can opener on the counter. Dad came home for lunch, saw that Mom was gone, and no lunch was made.

He promptly came to our house and remarked, "I'll show her. I just won't eat."

My husband said, "That's right! You'll just starve yourself to death and that'll show her!"

Dad said, "Yeah."

Then, they both started laughing and Dad went hungry until supper time.

~Edy Phelps~ (in remembrance of her father, Clifford Hirchert, her mother, Ethel Hirchert, and her husband, Robert Phelps)

Gravy

Back in the early 1960's when I was a teenager my mom decided to go to work and my dad had to eat what I cooked for him. He lost weight and so did I. Some of the stuff I came up with was so sad. My dad ate most of it without complaint. One day, my gravy was so thick that he had to cut it with a knife. He said it was a little chewy, but it had good flavor.

~Edy Phelps~

Main Dishes

Jerky

Cut meat into 1 1/4 inch strips

Soak in solution:

1 cup salt

1 quart warm water

1 cup liquid smoke

Drain well and sprinkle with pepper.

Turn oven to low setting and cook for 3 hours, turning the meat over half way through cooking time. Turn oven off and cool in the oven.

Prime Rib Roast

Approximately 6 to 8 pounds beef rib roast

2 teaspoon grated lemon peel

2 cloves garlic, crushed

1 teaspoon salt

1 teaspoon cracked black pepper

1 teaspoon dried rosemary leaves, crushed

Combine lemon peel, garlic, salt, pepper, and rosemary; rub evenly over surface of rib roast. Place roast, fat side up, on rack in sallow roasting pan. Insert meat thermometer into thickest part of roast, not touching bone or fat. Do not add water. Do not cover. Roast in 325°F (slow) oven to desired degree of doneness. Allow 23 to 25 minutes per pound for rare; 27 to 30 minutes per pound for medium. Cover roast with aluminum foil tent and allow to stand 15 to 20 minutes. Roast will continue to rise approximately 5°F to reach 140°F for rare; 160°F for medium.

Gram's Summer Sausage

Gram's Summer Sausage can be made with half venison and half ground beef. My family likes eating it as a snack. This recipe came from my mother-in-law. She could make anything taste good. Her left-overs were always a big treat for everyone. She made lunch meats from left-over roasts that were always great.

~Edy Phelps~ about Grandma June.

2 pounds Hamburger

3 Tablespoon Morton Quick Salt

1/4 teaspoon Garlic

1/4 teaspoon Onion

1/4 teaspoon Mustard seed

1/4 teaspoon Cracked pepper

1 cup Water

Mix with hands. Make into rolls and refrigerate for 24 hours. Cook at 350°F for 1 to 1 1/2 hours, drain juice.

Prize Winning Meat Loaf

1 1/2 pounds Lean ground beef

1 cup Tomato sauce

3/4 cup Quaker oats

1 Egg, slightly beaten

1/4 cup Onion, chopped

1/4 cup Green pepper, chopped

1/2 teaspoon salt

1/4 teaspoon Pepper

Heat oven to 350°F. Combine all ingredients; mix lightly but throughly. Press into 8 x 4 inch loaf pan. Bake 1 hour. Juices should run clear. Drain, let stand 5 minutes before serving.

One Step Lasagna

1 1/2 cup Water

1 16 oz. jar Spaghetti sauce

1 16 oz. box Lasagna noodles

1 container 15 oz. ricotta cheese or Cottage Cheese

8 oz. Mozzarella cheese

1/2 cup grated Parmesan

Preheat oven to 350°F. Combine 1 1/2 cup water with spaghetti sauce in bowl. Cover bottom of 13 x 9 x 2 baking dish with 1 1/2 cup sauce. Arrange layer of uncooked noodles, slightly overlapping on top of sauce. Spread 1/2 the ricotta or cottage cheese and 1/2 the mozzarella over noodles. Sprinkle with 2 Tablespoons parmesan. Add another layer of sauce. Bake for 1 hour.

Breads

Muffins

Pastry

Aunt Reesa

I remember as a small child, Aunt Reesa coming to visit. (My Dad's Aunt.) We all enjoyed her visits except I thought it was a little unfair that I always had to sleep with her. She snored, had whiskers and used my pillow. I asked my mother why she couldn't sleep with my brother. She told me, because he was a boy. I told her I didn't think it would make any difference if he wore his pajamas. Just because he was a boy it was my fate to sleep next to Aunt Reesa.

As I grew older and we moved from a mobile home into a house with a guest room I looked more forward to Aunt Reesa's yearly visit. I asked her on one occasion what she did for a living. She told me that she took care of elderly people. This was quite a shock since she was in her 70's at the time. She continued to care for the elderly until she was 85. She was quite a woman and one of the best cooks I ever knew. She could mix up a batch of banana bread like nobody's business.

~Edy Phelps~

Aunt Ressa's Banana Bread

1 pound Walnuts

1 pound Dates, chopped

1 jar Marashino cherries

6-8 large Bananas, mashed

5 Eggs

2 1/2 cups Sugar

2 cups Buttermilk

1 1/2 cups Vegetable oil

3/4 cup Molasses

1 teaspoon Salt

2 teaspoon Nutmeg

3 teaspoon Cinnamon

2 teaspoons Baking soda

3 teaspoons Baking powder

5 cups Flour

Mix the eggs, sugar, buttermilk, vegetable oil, molasses and salt. Beat well, then add bananas. Set aside. Mix well the nutmeg, cinnamon, baking soda, baking powder, and flour. Combine liquid ingredients into flour mixture. Add dates, cherries, and walnuts. Add more flour until quite stiff. Grease and flour 5 single loaf pans. Bake at 350°F for 50 minutes or until toothpick comes out clean.

Pumpkin Bread

1 1/2 cups Sugar

1/2 cup Salad oil

2 cups Flour

2 Eggs

1/2 cup Water

1 cup Pumpkin

1 teaspoon Baking soda

1/2 teaspoon Salt

1/2 teaspoon Cinnamon

1/2 teaspoon Cloves

1/2 teaspoon Nutmeg

1/2 cup Walnuts

Grease and flour 2 one pound loaf pans. Combine all ingredients. Bake at 350°F for 1 1/2 hours.

Rhubarb Muffins

1 14/ cups Brown sugar

1/2 cup Vegetable oil

2 teaspoon Vanilla

1 Egg

1 cup Milk

2 1/2 cups Flour

1/2 teaspoon Salt

1 1/2 cups Rhubarb, chopped

1 teaspoon Baking soda

1 teaspoon Baking powder

1/2 cup Walnuts

Combine all ingredients. Place about 1/4 cup in muffin cups. Sprinkle tops with cinnamon and sugar. Bake at 350°F for 20 minutes.

Tarts

Shells:

3 oz. Cream cheese

1/2 cup Butter

1 cup Flour

Filling:

1 Egg, slightly beaten

3/4 cup Brown sugar

2 cups Butter

1 teaspoon Vanilla

1 cup Nuts (pecans)

Cream together shell ingredients. Form into mini muffin tins; approximately 1 Tablespoon per shell. Mix together the ingredients for the filling, then add 3/4 teaspoon filling into each shell. Bake at 325°F for 25-30 minutes.

Homemade Bread on the Ranch

When I was between the ages of four and eight, my family lived on a ranch in western South Dakota. There was always a lot of extra work to do, especially when it came to calving and branding time. We had hired hands that lived in a bunkhouse close by. They helped out with all of the ranch work, but my mom, by herself, had to cook everyday, three times a day, for all of these men. Sometimes up to twelve extra men. One thing I remember the best about that time was the smell of hot, freshly baked bread coming out of the old cook stove. My brother and I were always the first in line for that first teaming slice with homemade butter spread on the top.

Mom always said that while kneading the dough, if it popped and squeaked, you had good bread dough. (Unfortunately, I have never quite mastered my mom's bread.) After the dough would rise, she would cut off a few pieces and fry it until it was golden brown and roll it in sugar for us. This was a real treat. Mom called these dough guards. Some people call them Elephant ears, Donkey ears, or fried bread dough. Whatever the correct name for them, they were always delicious.

~Edy Phelps~

Bread

1 Medium potato, boiled

1/2 cup Sugar

5 cups Potato water

2 packages Dry yeast

1 cup Lukewarm water

1 teaspoon Sugar

6 plus cups Flour

2 Tablespoons Lard

2 teaspoon Salt

Dissolve yeast in 1 cup lukewarm water and 1 teaspoon sugar. Boil one medium potato in 5 cups of water. Mash the potato in the water. Add in 1/2 cup sugar while water is still hot. Let cool then add yeast mixture. Pour this liquid into the flour, lard, and salt. Add enough flour to make a soft dough. Knead to a medium dough. Let rise twice. The third time, shape into loaves. Makes six loaves. Let rise in pans until double in size. Bake at 350°F for 1 hour.

Jiffy White Buns

1 package Dry yeast

1/2 cup Lukewarm milk

1/2 cup Lukewarm water

1 teaspoon Salt

1/2 teaspoon Sugar

3 Tablespoons Shortening

3 Tablespoons Sugar

3 cups White flour

1 Egg, well beaten

Combine yeast, lukewarm water, and sugar and let proof for 10-15 minutes. Combine yeast mixture, egg, and flour. Then, mix in, in this order, milk, salt, sugar, and shortening. Let rise until double in size, then shape into buns and let rise again. Bake at 375°F for 15-20 minutes.

We always had hot buns for holiday dinners. Especially if we were having turkey. My favorite part of these special occasions were the cold turkey sandwiches after the meal.
~Edy Phelps~

Buns

2 packages Dry yeast

1/2 cup Lukewarm water

1 cup Sugar

2 teaspoon Salt

1 quart Milk

3 Eggs, beaten

1 cup Cooking oil

6 cups Flour

Dissolve the yeast in 1/2 cup water. Boil the milk and let cool. Add the yeast mixture, eggs, and sugar. Mix in the cooking oil and salt. Knead in flour; enough to make a soft dough. Let rise. Knead down and let rise again. Shape into buns and place on a greased pan. Let rise until double in size. Bake at 375°F for 12-15 minutes.

Substitutions

It is so disconcerting when you are baking to run out of or be out of something just when you are in the middle of mixing up your favorite recipe. This is when you should remember to be kind to those around you because there is only one substitution to so many things, such as cinnamon or sugar. That substitution is my neighbor's instead of mine. I have to admit I had some great neighbors.

I love you Ging. Thanks for all the times you met me at the fence.

It's also not always recommended to try and replace what you can buy in the grocery store with your own version. For example, I was out of crackers one day and was looking through one of my old cookbooks and found a soda cracker recipe. I mixed up a batch with great expectations. *Wow, I can make my own soda crackers and save millions.*

I have one suggestion for those soda crackers. If you can't afford soda crackers, you might as well eat dirt. It would probably go down just as easily with more nutrition and wouldn't be quite as dry. A little bit of water with dirt makes mud. A little bit of water with those soda crackers, "ewwwww" you don't want to know what that made.

Desserts

I used to cook Brown Sugar Frosting at home as a teenager. I always used one of Mom's rubber spatulas, and she always had to replace it after I got done melting it. So, my suggestion is to use a wooden spoon instead. This frosting is great on spice cake.

~Edy Phelps~

Brown Sugar Frosting

Melt over low heat: 1/4 cup Butter

3/4 cup Brown sugar

Add: 3 Tablespoons milk

Bring to a full boil for two minutes, stirring constantly. Cool.

Add: 2 cups Powdered sugar

1/2 teaspoon Vanilla

Beat until smooth. Now it's ready to frost your cake.

Chocolate Frosting

6 Tablespoon Milk

1 1/2 cup Sugar

6 Tablespoon Butter

1/4 package Chocolate chips

Boil 1 minute, then add 1/4 package chocolate chips.

Penuche Frosting

3 Tablespoon Butter

1/4 cup Milk

1 cup Light brown sugar (packed)

1 teaspoon Vanilla

1 3/4 cups Powdered sugar

Over low heat melt the butter. Add milk and brown sugar. Cook over low heat, stirring constantly, for three minutes. Cool. Add vanilla and about 1 3/4 cup powdered sugar. Beat until smooth.

Rich Cocoa Fudge

3 cups Sugar

1 1/2 cups Milk

2/3 cup Cocoa

1/4 cup Butter

1/4 teaspoon Salt

1 teaspoon Vanilla

Line 8 or 9 inch square pan with foil; butter foil. In heavy 4 quart saucepan, stir together sugar, coca, and salt; stir in milk. Cook over medium heat, stirring constantly until mixture comes to full roiling boil. Boil without stirring to 234°F or until syrup, when dropped into very cold water, forms a soft ball which flattens when removed from water. Remove from heat. Add butter and vanilla; DO NOT STIR. Cool at room temperature to 110°F (lukewarm). Beat with wooden spoon until fudge thickens and loses some of its gloss. Spread quickly into prepared pan; cool. Cut into squares.

Peanut Butter Fudge

2 cups White sugar

1/4 cup Peanut butter

1/4 cup Corn syrup

1 Tablespoon Butter

1/2 cup Milk or water

1 teaspoon Vanilla

3 Tablespoon cocoa

Combine all ingredients, except vanilla, into a saucepan and let boil five minutes. Cool. Add vanilla and beat. Pour into an 8 or 9 inch square pan. Let set up then cut and serve.

Festive Fudge

3 cups Chocolate chips

1 14 oz. can Sweetened Condensed Milk

Dash of Salt

1 1/2 teaspoon Vanilla

1/2 to 1 cup nuts, optional

Melt chips over low heat with sweetened condensed milk and salt. Remove from heat, stir in nuts and vanilla. Spread evenly into wax paper lined 8 or 9 inch square pan. Chill tow hours or until firm.

Rhubarb Fool

1 1/2 pounds Rhubarb

1/4 cup Water

1 1/2 cup Sugar

1 cup Whipped cream

Cut the rhubarb into 2 inch lengths and combine with sugar and water in a heavy 2-quart saucepan. Cover and simmer until the rhubarb is quite tender - about 30 minutes. When cool, chill and blend in a blender and fold into whipped cream. Serve very cold.

Jelly Roll

4 Eggs

1 cup Sugar

1 cup Sifted flour

1 teaspoon Baking powder

4 Tablespoons Cold water

1 teaspoon Vanilla

Pinch of Salt

Beat eggs well. Add water and stir. Add dry ingredients. Add vanilla and stir well. Pour into well buttered 9 x 15 inch pan. Bake 15 minutes at 375°F. Turn out onto damp cloth. Sprinkle with powdered sugar. Spread with jelly and roll up. Slice into pieces.

Easy Cinnamon Rolls

3 tubes biscuits

1/2 cup Brown sugar

1/4 cup Milk

1/2 cup Butter or margarine

1 cup White sugar

2 teaspoon Cinnamon

Grease a bundt pan or one-piece angle food pan. Mix brown sugar and milk and pour into pan. Place biscuits on edge in pan. Mix the butter, sugar and cinnamon and pour over the top of biscuits. Bake at 350°F for about 30 minutes.

Fruit Punch Bars

2 1/4 cups Flour

2 Eggs

1 1/2 cup Sugar

1 1/3 cup Coconut

17 oz. can Fruit cocktail with juice

1 1/2 teaspoon Baking soda

1/2 teaspoon salt

1 teaspoon Vanilla

1/2 cup Walnuts

Beat eggs and sugar until fluffy. Add rest of ingredients except coconut and nuts. Grease and flour 11 x 14 inch deep dish cookie sheet. Pour batter into pan. Sprinkle coconut and nuts on top. Bake at 350°F for 20 minutes or until toothpick comes out clean.

Topping:

3/4 cup Sugar

1/2 cup Butter

1/4 cup Evaporated milk

1/2 teaspoon Vanilla

Boil ingredients for 2 minutes. Remove from heat and drizzle over warm bars.

Lemon Squares

2 cups Flour

1 cup Butter

1/2 cup Powdered sugar

Mix together and press in bottom of pan. Bake at 350°F for 25 minutes or until light brown.

4 Eggs

2 cups Sugar

1 teaspoon Baking powder

1/2 teaspoon Salt

4 Tablespoons Lemon juice

Beat remaining ingredients until light and fluffy. Pour over hot crust. Bake at 350°F for 20 minutes. No imprint should remain when touched.

Brownie Mix for Storing

5 cups Flour

4 teaspoon Baking powder

4 teaspoon Salt

8 cups Sugar

2 1/2 cups Cocoa

2 cups Shortening

Mix first flour, baking powder, and salt. Set aside. Mix the sugar and cocoa together and then add to the flour mixture. Cut in shortening. Stores for 6 weeks.

To bake:

2 cups Brownie Mix

2 Eggs

1 teaspoon Vanilla

2/3 cups Nuts

Blend well. Batter will not be smooth. Bake at 350°F in an 8 x 8 inch pan for 20 to 25 minutes.

Dump Cake

1 box Yellow or white cake mix

1/2 cup (one stick) Butter

1 can Cherries for pie

1 can Crushed pineapple

In a 13 x 9 inch pan mix together the can of cherries and the crushed pineapple. Do not drain. Spread the dry cake mix over the top of the fruit mixture. Cut the butter into pats and place over the top of the cake mix. Bake in a 350°F oven for one hour.

You can substitute other fruits for this recipe. I've used strawberries and pineapple, for example. This is a great recipe to experiment with.

Glorified Rice

1 box Lemon Jello

1 8 oz. container of Cool Whip

6 cups Cooked rice

1 can Crushed pineapple

Cook the Jello as per the instructions on the box. Let cool but not fully set up. Cook enough rice to make 6 cups. Let cool. Add the rice and pineapple to the Jello and mix well. Refrigerate until Jello has set up or over night. Add in the Cool Whip just before serving.

In Conclusion

I have had a great time writing all of this down. It brought back so many great memories. If anybody ever tells you nothing is forever, just remind them of all the memories they have passed onto their children and that their children will pass onto their children. Then tell them, yes, memories are forever. I guess that's where the word history comes from

~Edy Phelps~

Mom has so many other recipes that I hope to compile into this book over time. I'm afraid most of her usual "stand-bys" as she calls them, were in her head. I have added in several that she didn't have written down, but had taught me over the years. Most of them are desserts as that's my favorite part of any meal. I mainly wanted to get out the most important part of this cookbook... her thoughts.

~JC Phelps~

Printed in Great Britain
by Amazon